Contents

Any words appearing in bold, **like this**, are explained in the Glossary.

Who were the ancient Greeks?

Much of Greece is covered by mountains. This made it hard to travel around by land in ancient times. But Greece also has sea on three sides, in which there are many islands. So the sea was always important to the ancient Greeks. They travelled by sea as much as they could. This meant they needed **harbours** to land in. Some of these harbours grew into **ports** – places where ships came from all over ancient Greece. Ports were especially useful to **traders**, because they could meet there to trade.

Look for these:
The ship shows you the subject of each chapter. The picture of an amphora shows you boxes with interesting facts, figures, and quotes about life in a Greek port.

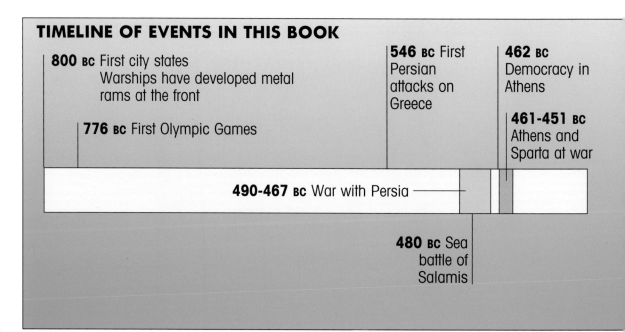

TIMELINE OF EVENTS IN THIS BOOK

800 BC First city states
Warships have developed metal rams at the front

776 BC First Olympic Games

546 BC First Persian attacks on Greece

462 BC Democracy in Athens

461–451 BC Athens and Sparta at war

490–467 BC War with Persia

480 BC Sea battle of Salamis

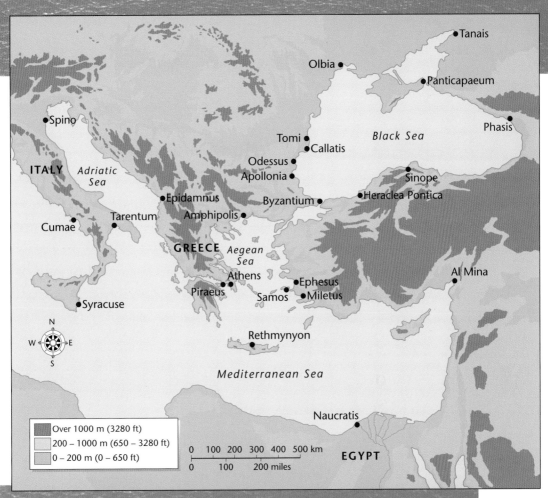

This map of ancient Greece shows how the sea broke it up into islands and bays. You can see why ships and ports were so important to the ancient Greeks.

146 BC Romans take over Greece.

0

A safe harbour

All ships needed a safe **harbour** – a place on the coast to keep them safe at night, or in bad weather. Fishermen and their families lived in villages by harbours. Some harbours grew into busy **ports**. They had to be big enough to hold a lot of ships and be in easy reach of cities and other ports. Sailors and people who worked in **trade** and their families lived and worked there. Other people came there to trade.

PIRAEUS

Piraeus was probably one of the first places used as a safe harbour for Athens. From 493 BC on it grew into a port with its own **warehouses** and **docks**. Later, it became a bigger town with a theatre and **temples**, too. The road from Piraeus to Athens had high walls on each side, to make it safe.

Even today, many Greek islands can only be reached by sea. A safe harbour is still important.

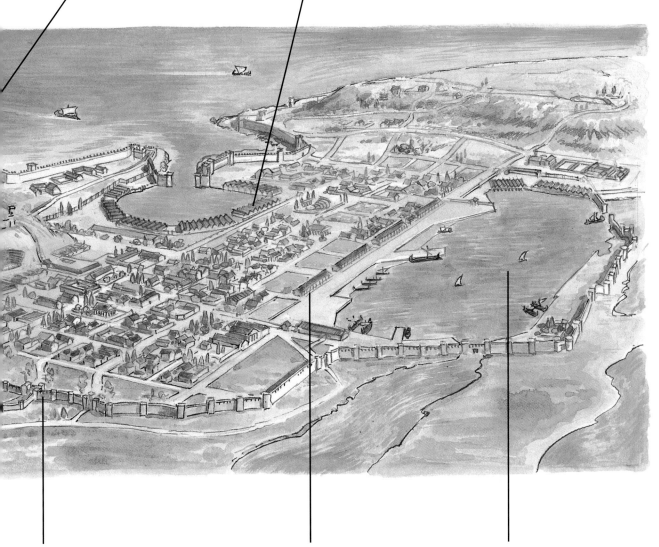

There was a third harbour for fighting ships just a little way along the coast.

These sheds were used to store and repair fighting ships.

High stone walls protected the port.

Traders stored their goods in these warehouses.

This harbour was used by trading ships and fighting ships.

How ships were built

Shipbuilders made ships of different sizes and shapes, depending on what they were used for. Warships were long, to fit lots of people in. They were light and low, to move quickly through the water. They needed oars, to row if there was no wind. **Trade** ships did not need to be fast. They had to hold a lot of **cargo**. So they had high sides and fewer oars.

TOOLS

Shipmakers used simple wooden tools. Any metal cutting edges were made from **bronze** or iron. The most important ship building tools were:

- a saw (to cut the wood)
- a hammer and chisel (to shape it)
- a plane (to smooth it).

These are some of the kinds of simple wooden tools a ship's carpenter would have used.

Shipmakers shaped the **keel** first. This was the long, thick piece of wood that ran along the bottom of the ship, in the middle. They made the outside frame by joining planks of wood tightly together, joined to the keel. Once the outside was finished, shipbuilders nailed planks across the inside, to strengthen it. They painted the outside with **tar** to make it waterproof.

Many ships had a sail for using the wind. The sail hung from a mast in the middle of the ship.

Where ships sailed

The ancient Greeks knew that the sea was full of dangers. Ships had to face storms and **pirates**. If bad weather blew them out to sea, they might get lost because they had no proper maps or instruments to help them **navigate**. But the ancient Greeks wanted to **trade** and to set up **colonies** – settlements of Greeks in other lands. So they went to sea despite the dangers.

This map shows how the Greek **city states** set up colonies around the coast of the Mediterranean Sea and into the Black Sea. They traded in all these places and got there by following the line of the coast.

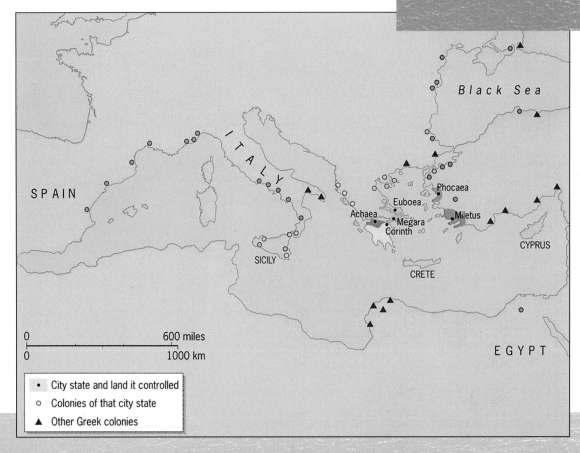

Black Sea

SPAIN

ITALY

Phocaea

Euboea

Achaea

Megara
Corinth

Miletus

CYPRUS

SICILY

CRETE

EGYPT

0   600 miles
0   1000 km

• City state and land it controlled
○ Colonies of that city state
▲ Other Greek colonies

To navigate sailors tried to keep land always in sight. This is why they travelled mainly by daylight, landing at night if they could. Some sailors travelled to the same places a lot, so knew the shape of the land and how long it took to get from one place to another. At other times, sailors asked in **ports** until they found someone who could tell them the way.

SAILING FURTHER

One Greek traveller, Pythias, got as far as Britain, and wrote about his experiences. Historians think he got there by sailing to southern Spain in Greek ships. But Greek ships did not sail all the way to Britain. So after getting to Spain, he probably got a ride with other ships.

We can find out where the ancient Greeks sailed to in many ways. This make-up pot shows a lion. It comes from the other side of the Mediterranean, near North Africa.

11

Sailors

There were not many full-time sailors. **Citizens** of the **city state** rowed and fought in the warships. Ships that went exploring or to **trade** often had some **experienced** sailors on board. Rich traders often hired an experienced captain and crew to sail their ships. But this cost a lot. Smaller traders, just starting out, sometimes bought a ship with friends. Often, these small traders sailed the ship themselves.

Stories of the dangers sailors faced told of storms and **pirates**. They also talked about imaginary creatures sent by the gods. The **sirens** on this vase sang to make sailors sail their ships on to rocks, wrecking them.

Sailors did not spend all their time at sea. Spring and summer were the best times for sailing, as the weather was better. So sailors often had a second job, to do when they were not at sea. If they lived in a **port**, their job was often to do with the sea. They could make ropes, sails or nets, or build and repair boats.

STAYING HOME

The ancient Greek writer Hesiod described how sailors laid their boats up in winter: "Drag your ship up the shore and pack stones all around to hold it firm. Take the plug out of the bottom, so rain does not collect in it and rot it. Store the sails, rope and tackle in your house and hang the steering rudder high in the roof above the fire."

This vase painting shows young men diving for sponges that grew naturally on the sea bed.

Traders

Some people in **trade** sold just one thing, such as **grain**. Other traders sold a mix of different things. They chose the **goods** they thought would make them the most money. Wine, oil, and grain were most often traded. A ship sunk near Cyprus in about 350 BC was carrying 404 jars of wine, about 10,000 almonds in sacks and 29 millstones, to use for grinding corn.

This vase has a picture of a man buying fish from a fish monger. There were no fridges or freezers in ancient Greece, so fish was sold the day it was caught.

Many traders borrowed money to buy goods to trade. They hoped to make enough money to pay back the borrowed money, and the extra the **banker** charged for lending it, and still have some money left over. The banker sometimes agreed not to ask for the money back if the ship sank.

A TRADER'S TRICK

A trader called Hegestratos borrowed money to buy grain to trade. He did not buy grain, but kept the money and sailed the ship away empty. He made a hole in the ship, to sink it. His banker would not ask for the money back if the ship sank. But when Hegestratos jumped overboard he could not find his escape boat. He drowned. The sailors mended the hole, and got the ship home, and the trick was discovered.

Each Greek **city state** had different coins. The countries outside Greece had different coins again. So Greek traders needed to work with bankers who could swap different kinds of coins.

Warehouses and docks

Ports needed space in the **harbour** for ships to dock and **warehouses** near the **docks**, so traders could store their **goods**. A large port, like Piraeus, often had two docks. There was a dock for warships with sheds to store them in. There was a bigger dock for trading ships. This did not have ship sheds, but it had warehouses all around it.

SHIP SHEDS

The **city state** of Athens had hundreds of warships, which were kept in sheds so that they stayed dry and could be repaired easily. The sheds had a stone ramp sloping down into the water for each ship. Slaves or donkeys pulled the ships up and down these ramps on ropes.

Warehouses were locked and guarded against thieves. Traders who bought and sold really precious goods, like this gold jewellery, often stored them at home, not at the docks.

Most traders had several **slaves** working at their warehouse, loading and unloading. Unlike many Greek buildings, warehouses had solid walls on all sides, and no windows. They had to keep the goods inside dry and also keep out thieves and animals. If mice or rats got into a grain warehouse, they could eat and spoil all the grain inside very quickly.

Traders could sell Greek marble and stone statues for a lot of money. But they were hard to move and heavy to carry by boat. If a statue was dropped during loading it could sink a ship before it even set sail.

Warships

The first Greek warships sailed close enough to each other for those on board to fight using their hands. By 800 BC, the Greeks were using a ram – a heavy lump of metal on the front of the ship. They sailed at the enemy ships, hoping to make holes in the side that were big enough to sink them. Over time, the Greeks built their ships with two, then three, levels of rowers, to make them faster and quicker at escaping the enemy. The ships must have been very crowded.

This vase painting shows an early warship, with just one row of oars on each side.

In 480 BC, the Persians invaded Greece, and won several land battles. Their army and **navy** headed for Athens. The Athenian navy trapped the Persians and beat them. A Greek playwright wrote a Persian view of the battle: "The Greeks made a circle around us and rammed holes in our ships. You could not see the water, it was so full of wrecked ships and dead men."

This is a modern artist's idea of how the Greek ships moved towards the trapped Persian ships during the 480 BC invasion.

Pirates and explorers

Usually people went to sea to fish, to **trade**, or to fight. But other kinds of people went to sea, such as **pirates** and explorers. Pirates usually lived and worked from an island not too far from the coast. Pirates had their own rules. They did not usually rob ships from their own **city state**. They robbed pirates from other city states and trading ships.

This vase painting shows a pirate ship attacking a trading ship. The pirate ship, on the right, was designed like a warship. You can see the ram on the front, getting closer to the trading ship.

Alexander had thought that Nearchus and his men were dead. He was surprised to see them back. They were sunburned and tired. One Greek historian wrote, "Their hair was long and tangled. Their bodies were thin and dirty. But they were alive".

Part of a huge statue of Poseidon, god of the sea. Ancient Greek sailors believed Poseidon could send them calm seas or storms.

The ancient Greeks who went exploring were usually sent by the leaders of their city state. The most famous Greek explorer was called Nearchus. Alexander the Great, the first person to rule all of Greece, sent him exploring in 325 BC. Nearchus took about 100 ships and explored the Indian Ocean for about a year. His sailors, used to the calmer Mediterranean Sea, were terrified by the waves and got very seasick.

Family life

Sailors and their families usually had a home in the **port**. They lived like other Greeks, the women staying at home while the men went out to work. Greek women were usually expected to stay indoors most of the time, while their husbands did the shopping. But sailors' wives were left alone when their husbands went to sea. So, in ports, women sent a **slave** to shop, or shopped together in groups.

While their husbands were gone, women did the same duties they did when their husbands were at home. They spun wool, wove cloth, and brought up the children. This woman is making a funeral wreath.

22

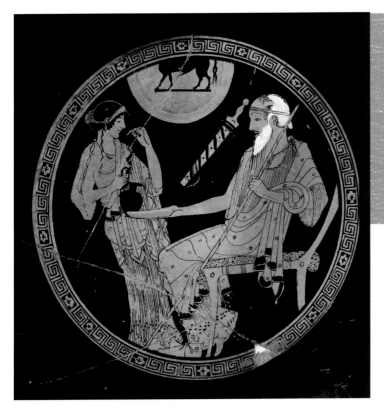

Most ancient Greeks had at least one slave to do the housework and serve the meals. Men ate separately from women.

SLAVES

A man who could afford to keep a slave but who did not was seen as mean. This was the kind of person this Greek writer laughs at: "When he shops, he carries the meat from the market himself, in his hands, and the vegetables in the fold of his cloak. He stays indoors when his clothes are at the laundry [because he is too mean to buy a change of clothes]."

Rich traders often did not live in the port. They lived in the city. A slave ran the business for them, although the traders visited from time to time to check on things. Poorer traders lived in the port, but as they did not always sail on trading trips, they did not leave their families for long periods of time.

Travelling

Ships were used for fighting and to **trade**, but they also took passengers. People did not travel, either on foot or by boat, unless they had to. They might travel to see a sick relative, or to go to a **religious festival** in the nearest town. They travelled short distances in local fishing boats. For longer distances, they had to find a trading ship going in the right direction.

This vase shows the god Dionysus asleep on the deck of a ship. Sleeping on deck was uncomfortable, but sleeping below the deck, where the **goods** were stored, was both uncomfortable and airless.

Travellers got to the nearest **port** on foot, on a cart or riding a donkey. This depended on how far they had to go and how rich they were. All travel was dirty, dangerous, and uncomfortable. On ships, travellers and sailors slept on deck if they could not land at night. If they could land at night, they slept on the beach.

WHERE TO STAY

Travellers could not always leave the port as soon as they arrived. They had to find a ship going in the right direction. If they could, people stayed with family or friends. If not, they stayed at an **inn**. This gave them a bed for the night, but most inns (travellers complained at the time) were not comfortable or clean.

Ancient Greeks who set out on important journeys often wanted to know if they would come back safely. This soldier is looking at the insides of a bird he has sacrificed to the gods. The Greeks believed this could tell the future.

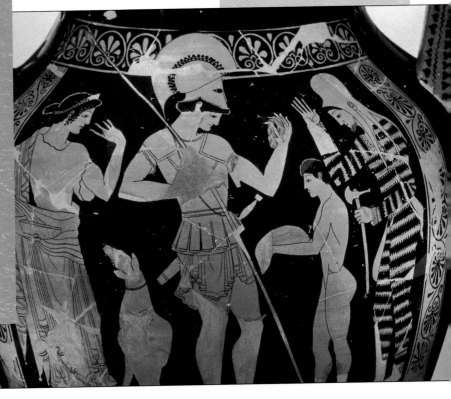

Food and drink

Ancient Greek sailors, fighters and explorers ate and drank what they could, when they could. If they landed at night, they slept and cooked on the beach. Often they ate very little but the fish they caught, with maybe some herbs they found from the land around the beach.

Sailors cooked directly over, or in, the fires they lit on the beach. The fires also helped to keep them warm at night.

Coriander fish

The ancient Greeks ate much more fish than meat. They grilled many fish whole, but sometimes they baked them in a pot on the fire, as they would have done with the fish in this recipe.

You will need:
2 fillets of white fish, such as haddock or cod
2 tablespoons of coriander seeds
1 teaspoon of salt
vegetable oil
some white wine vinegar

1 Heat the oven to 190°C (375°F).

2 Bake the coriander seeds on a baking sheet for 10 minutes. Leave them to cool. Put them with the salt in a plastic food bag and use a heavy rolling pin to crush them down a bit.

3 Put the fish in an oven dish that has been oiled with the cooking oil.

4 Sprinkle the salt and coriander over the fish.

5 Cover the dish with foil and bake in the oven for 20 minutes.

6 Remove from the oven and sprinkle the vinegar over the fish.

Free time

People who lived in Greek **ports** spent their free time in the same way as other ancient Greeks. The men spent most of their time outside, especially in the summer, when the heat made homes hot. They exercised, ate and drank, and gambled. Women spent their time together, with their children.

FUN AT SEA?

We know that many ancient Greeks thought that sailing was dangerous. So they probably did not sail for pleasure, as people do today. We do know that they swam and fished for pleasure and exercise, especially men and boys.

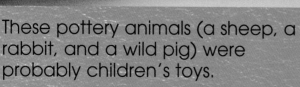
These pottery animals (a sheep, a rabbit, and a wild pig) were probably children's toys.

Babies and young children played with toys and with friends. But from the age of about seven, they had less and less free time. Girls had to help their mothers around the house, to learn how to run a home of their own. Boys either went to school or began to work with their father, learning his job.

This terracotta statue shows Greek women playing a game called knucklebones. This was played with cleaned animal bones, which is how the game got its name.

Glossary

banker person who lends money to people in return for getting extra money back

bronze metal made by melting copper and tin together

cargo goods to trade that are taken by sea

citizen man who is born in a city to parents who were citizens

city state a city and the land it controls around it

colonies settlements in one country set up by people from another country

dock part of a harbour where ships can stay for long periods of time

experienced someone who has done something a lot and knows how to do it very well

goods things that are made, bought, and sold

grain types of grasses with fat seeds that are eaten. Barley wheat, rye, oats, and rice are all grains.

harbour a sheltered place on the coast

inn houses where the owner rented out small rooms for people to sleep in for the night. Some inns also fed people.

keel the long, thick piece of wood that runs along the bottom of the ship in the middle

navigate work out how to get from one place to another

navy ships used to fight for a country

pirates robbers that rob at sea

ports where ships come to trade or rest

religious festival several days of religious celebrations, usually held every year

sirens imaginary creatures with beautiful voices that sang to sailors to make them crash their ships and drown

slaves person who is bought and sold by someone and has to work for that person

tar black sticky substance that is waterproof

temple place where gods and goddesses are worshipped

trade this can mean:

1 job

2 selling or swapping goods

warehouse a place where goods are stored

Further resources

Books
Ancient Greece, Christine Hatt (Heinemann Library, 2004)
Explore History: Ancient Greece (Heinemann Library, 2001)
History in Art: Ancient Greece, Andrew Langley (Raintree, 2004)
The Ancient Greeks, Pat Taylor (Heinemann Library, 1994)
What families were like: Ancient Greece, Alison Cooper
(Hodder Wayland, 2001)
Worldwise: Ancient Greeks, Daisy Kerr (Franklin Watts, 1997)
You are in Ancient Greece, Ivan Minnis (Raintree, 2004)

Websites
www.ancientgreece.com
A good website looking at all aspects of ancient Greek life.

www.historyforkids.org/learn/greeks
A useful website full of links and extra resources.

www.bbc.co.uk/schools/ancientgreece/main_menu.shtml
Use the games and interactive activities to find out more
about life in ancient Greece.

www.olympic.org/uk/games/ancient/index_uk.asp
Visit this website to find out all about the Olympics.

Disclaimer
All the Internet addresses (URLs) given in this book were valid at the time of going to
press. However, due to the dynamic nature of the Internet, some addresses may have
changed, or sites may have ceased to exist since publication. While the author and
publishers regret any inconvenience this may cause readers, no responsibility for any
such changes can be accepted by either the author or the publishers.

Index